C000205410

CHRISTMAS

WITH

Dickens

CHRISTMAS
WITH
Dickens

*Seasonal recipes inspired
by the life and work of
Charles Dickens*

Pen Vogler

CICO BOOKS

LONDON NEW YORK

Published in 2018 by CICO Books
An imprint of Ryland Peters & Small Ltd
20-21 Jockey's Fields, London WC1R 4BW
341 E 116th St,New York, NY 10029

www.rylandpeters.com

10 9 8 7 6 5 4 3 2 1

Printed in China

Editor: Gillian Haslam
Photographer: Ria Osborne
Stylist: Luis Peral
Food stylist: Ellie Jarvis

Art director: Sally Powell
Head of production: Patricia Harrington
Publishing manager: Penny Craig
Publisher: Cindy Richards

A CIP catalog record for this book is
available from the Library of Congress and
the British Library.

ISBN: 978 1 78249 645 8

NOTES:

All eggs are US large/UK medium unless
otherwise specified.

Both American (Imperial and US cups)
and British (metric) measurements are
included in these recipes. However, it is
important to work with only one set of
measurements and not to alternate
between the two within a recipe.

CONTENTS

Introduction 6

Lobster Patties 8

Pickled Salmon 10

Betsey Prig's Twopenny Salad 12

Roast Goose 14

Roast Fowl 18

Mashed and Brown Potatoes 21

Cauliflower with Parmesan 22

A Yorkshire Christmas Pie 24

Pickled Pork 25

Leicestershire Pork Pie 28

Chestnut and Apple Mince Pies 32

Christmas Pudding 34

Punch Sauce 37

Mr. Dick's Gingerbread 38

Twelfth Cake 40

Ladies' Fingers 44

Orange and Redcurrant Jellies 46

Charlotte Russe 50

French Plums 54

Wassail 56

Punch 58

Smoking Bishop 60

Bibliography 62

Index of Recipes 63

Acknowedgments 64

INTRODUCTION

Dickens' eldest daughter, Mamie, said that her father "loved Christmas for its deep significance as well as its joys." In a letter he once described the pleasures of Christmas with his family and friends as, "Such dinings, such dancings, such conjuring, such blind-man's buffing, such theatre-goings, such kissings-out of old years and kissings-in of new ones." Food and drink were part of the "joys" of Christmas but also part of its "deep significance" of charitable giving, taking responsibility for and showing love for one's fellow humans.

From Medieval times onward, decent landlords and farmers would have given their workers a Christmas bird or joint of meat. When families migrated to the cities in the Industrial Revolution and these links were broken, the urban poor found themselves with no benefactors. *A Christmas Carol*, which Dickens published in a white heat in 1843, brilliantly drew attention to their plight: the Cratchits were poor, hard-working, honest and a nuclear family— all aspects that Dickens' middle-class readers could identify with, particularly when combined with joyous Christmas scenes and the traditional Christmas ghost story, underscored with the theme of redemption.

The story's wild success has had the effect of anchoring a menu of seasonal food—turkey and pudding—to a single day. By contrast, in *Great Expectations* Dickens shows an old-fashioned rural feast of pickled pork and roast fowls. There is also supposed to be the "nice, round compact pork pie" that Pip has passed on to Magwitch, along with the Christmas mincemeat; an act of charitable giving for which Pip suffers enormously.

By the nineteenth century, advances in cattle breeding meant roast beef had overtaken venison as the meat with which the upper classes celebrated at Christmas, although the burly, fleshy turkey was beginning to be fashionable too. The urban poor paid into "goose clubs": the birds would be fattened in a back yard somewhere on the edge of the city, and at Christmas lots were drawn for each bird. It is no accident that Ebenezer Scrooge sees the Cratchit family enjoying a goose for their paltry Christmas Present, but he sends a boy off to buy them the luxury of a turkey.

Plum pudding, made with dried fruits, was a winter speciality for when the stores of apples, pears, and quinces were drying up and there

was no spring fruit yet. It didn't start to lose its old-fashioned name until two years after the publication of A Christmas Carol when the Dickens-loving cookbook writer Eliza Acton gives the first recipe for "Christmas Pudding." Its cousin, the Christmas Cake, started life as the great Twelfth Cake but it migrated to Christmas day when Twelfth Night was squeezed out of the calendar by Queen Victoria's disapproval of its riotousness, and the demands of big business to cut short the festive season.

Dickens was no friend of the temperance movement. He believed that the poor as well as the wealthy had the right to a sociable drink, and his Christmas stories are full of hot punch, Smoking Bishop (a delicious mulled port), and wassail of the sort that cheers and enlivens the riotous Christmas Eve party in The Pickwick Papers.

The festive recipes gathered here are inspired by Dickens' life and times and his profound belief that everybody has the right to good food and good company. I hope they bring you joy.

LOBSTER PATTIES

Paul Dombey's christening feast is a grand but icy occasion with its "cold fowls-ham-patties-salad-lobster". These lobster patties are luxurious and also warm—perfect for winter festivities.
Eliza Acton commends the Victorian patty (from the French for pastry) as an elegant and economical way of making lobster stretch further "at supper parties" and for using up leftover turkey, fowls, partridges, or pheasant.

12 oz/350g ready-made puff pastry

1 cup/250ml fish or chicken stock

1 level dessertspoon all-purpose/plain flour

1 cup/250ml light/single cream

a few drops of lemon juice

1 cooked hen lobster, meat chopped and coral set aside

MAKES 4 PATTIES

Preheat the oven to 400°F/200°C/Gas 6. Line a baking tray with baking parchment paper.

To make the pastry cases, roll out the pastry to ½ inch/12mm thick, taking care to keep it even so it rises evenly. Cut 2½-inch/6-cm circles and transfer them to the lined baking tray. Dip a 1¼-inch/3-cm cutter into very hot water and use it to cut halfway through the pastry. Bake in the preheated oven for 10–15 minutes until well risen and golden brown.

To make the lobster sauce, boil the stock to reduce it by half. In a bowl, mix the flour with a tablespoon of the cream, then stir in the rest of the cream. Gradually stir the warm stock into the cream mixture. Return it to the pan, add the lemon juice, and heat very gently, stirring all the time, for about 5 minutes, until it is a thick coating consistency. Take it off the heat. Crush the lobster coral (roe), add it to a tablespoon of the sauce, and beat them together well. Add this to the remainder of the white sauce and mix together. Add the chopped lobster meat.

Scoop out the lids of the patties using a sharp knife and trim the insides of the patties. Fill with the lobster sauce and serve warm.

This filling can be made with any fish or meat, using fish or meat stock as appropriate.

COMMON LOBSTER PATTIES

Prepare the fish as directed for fricasseed lobster, increasing a little the proportion of sauce. Fill the patty-cases with the mixture quite hot, and serve immediately.

Fricasseed Lobster: Take the flesh from the claws and tails of two moderate-sized lobsters, cut it into small scallops or dice; heat it slowly quite through in about three-quarters of a pint of good white sauce or béchamel; and serve it when it is at the point of boiling, after having stirred briskly to it a little lemon-juice just as it is taken from the fire.

Patty Cases: Roll out some of the lightest puff-paste to a half-inch of thickness, and with the larger of the tins cut the number of patties required; then dip the edge of the small shape into hot water, and press it about half through them. Bake them in a moderately quick oven from ten to twelve minutes, and when they are done, with the point of a sharp knife, take out the small rounds of crust from the tops, and scoop all the crumb from the inside of the patties, which may then be filled.

ELIZA ACTON, *Modern Cookery for Private Families*, 1845

PICKLED SALMON

Mrs. Gamp, in *Martin Chuzzlewit,* settles in to nurse her patient
by taking his pillows and ordering in "a little bit of pickled salmon,
with a nice little sprig of fennel, and a sprinkling of white pepper...."
This recipe brings together the best elements of pickled and fresh
salmon to make a light starter for a festive meal.

1¼ cups/300ml good-quality white wine vinegar

1¼ cups/300ml water

3 red onions, peeled and sliced

1 turnip, peeled, quartered, and roughly chopped

a bunch of flat-leaf parsley and thyme (tied together)

1 bay leaf

½ teaspoon salt

2–3 teaspoons sugar

12 whole white peppercorns, slightly crushed

1 lb 2 oz/500g salmon fillets, skinned

a handful of dill

For the dressing
reserved marinade

olive oil

Dijon or wholegrain mustard

To serve
sprigs of fennel, fennel flowers, or dill

SERVES 4 AS A MAIN COURSE
OR 8 AS AN APPETIZER

To make the marinade, put all the ingredients except the salmon and dill in a saucepan and bring to the boil. Simmer for 10–15 minutes, then put through a strainer/sieve, keeping the marinade.

Reserve 4–7 tablespoons/50–100ml of the marinade for a salad dressing.

If you wish to poach the salmon, put the strained marinade back in the pan, lower the fish into it, and let it simmer gently for 8–10 minutes, then set aside to cool.

For salmon that is a little raw and soft in the middle, place the salmon fillets in a glass or ceramic dish in a single layer and pour the hot marinade over them. Set aside to cool.

When the liquid is tepid, add the dill to the marinade. Chill in the fridge for 2 hours.

Remove the salmon from the marinade. Using a sharp knife, slice the fish thinly. Arrange on a plate, decorated with fennel sprigs, fennel flowers, or dill.

Serve with Betsey Prig's Twopenny Salad (see page 12). For the dressing, whisk the reserved marinade together with olive oil (in the ratio of 3 parts oil to 1 part marinade) and a little mustard.

TROUT A LA TWICKENHAM

The remains of trout, salmon, or mackerel, are excellent pickled: – put three onions in slices in a stewpan, with two ounces of butter, one turnip, a bouquet of parsley, thyme, and bay-leaf, pass them five minutes over the fire, add a pint of water and a pint of vinegar, two teaspoonfuls of salt and one of pepper, boil until the onions are tender, then strain it through a sieve over the fish; it will keep some time if required, and then do to pickle more fish by boiling over again.

ALEXIS SOYER, *The Modern Housewife or Ménagère*, 1849

BETSEY PRIG'S TWOPENNY SALAD

When Mrs. Gamp invites her friend Betsey Prig to tea, "two pounds of Newcastle salmon, intensely pickled" is on the menu; Mrs. Prig contributes as much salad as she can fit into her pocket, consisting of "either the oldest of lettuces or youngest of cabbages," shut up like an umbrella, mustard and cress, dandelion, radish, onion, beets/beetroot, and celery. Catherine also served beetroot and celery salads year round.

crisp lettuce such as Little Gem or Romaine

endive, chicory, radicchio, arugula/ rocket, or young dandelions or similar bitter leaves

6–8 radishes, thinly sliced

2–3 medium beets/beetroot, freshly boiled or baked, peeled and chopped into small cubes

4–6 salad onions or chives, finely chopped

4–5 stalks of heart celery, finely chopped

mustard and cress or soft herbs such as flat-leaf parsley or cilantro/ coriander

salad dressing, made with 5 parts oil to 2 parts cucumber or tarragon vinegar, plus salt and pepper (and optional sugar to taste)

SERVES 4 AS A MAIN COURSE OR 8 AS AN APPETIZER

Make the vinegar for the dressing by steeping cucumber or tarragon in good white wine vinegar or cider vinegar for around 3 hours.

Wash all the salad leaves and refresh in cold water if necessary. Shred the leaves and toss with the radish onto a salad bowl or plate. Sprinkle the chopped beet/beetroot, salad onions, and celery over. Decorate with chopped herbs or mustard and cress, and dress just before serving.

ENGLISH SALADS

The herbs and vegetables for a salad cannot be too freshly gathered; they should be carefully cleared from insects and washed with scrupulous nicety; they are better when not prepared until near the time of sending them to table, and should not be sauced until the instant before they are served.

Tender lettuces, of which the stems should be cut off, and the outer leaves be stripped away, mustard and cress, young radishes, and occasionally chives or small green onions (when the taste of a party is in favour of these last) are the usual ingredients of summer salads. (In early spring, the young white leaves of the dandelion will supply a very wholesome and excellent salad, of which the slight bitterness is to many persons as agreeable as that of the endive.) Half-grown cucumbers sliced thin, and mixed with them are a favourite addition with many persons. In England it is customary to cut the lettuces extremely fine; the French, who object to the flavour of the knife, which they fancy this mode imparts, break them small instead. Young celery alone, sliced and dressed with a rich salad mixture, is excellent; it is still in some families served thus always with roast pheasants.

Beet root, baked or boiled, blanched endive, small salad-herbs which are easily raised at any time of the year, celery, and hardy lettuces, with any ready-dressed vegetable, will supply salads through the winter. Cucumber vinegar is an agreeable addition to these.

ELIZA ACTON, Modern Cookery for Private Families, 1845

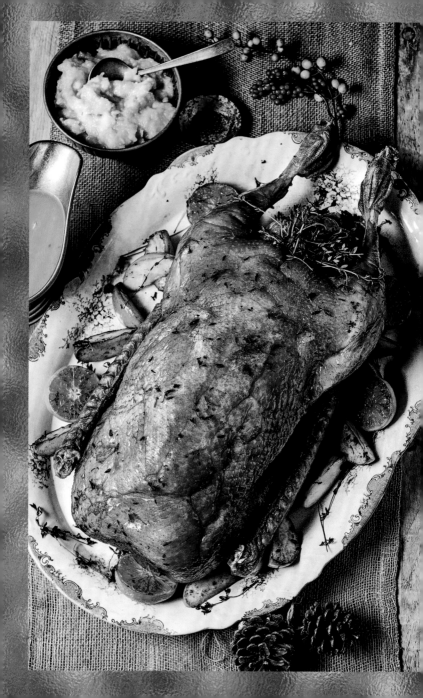

ROAST GOOSE

Poor families would ensure that they got their Christmas goose by paying into a goose club and, without an oven, having it roasted by the baker. In *A Christmas Carol*, the Cratchit children go wild outside the bakery at the smell of sage-and-onion stuffing, and the whole family admire their goose's flavor (and cheapness); Mrs. Cratchit ekes it out with apple sauce and mashed potatoes. A turkey, costlier and harder to buy in cities, is what the reformed Scrooge treats the Cratchit family to.

1 goose, about 11–13½ lb/5–6kg (with giblets and neck)

1 onion, peeled

a few sprigs of sage or thyme

For the stuffing

2 large onions, finely chopped

3 tablespoons freshly chopped sage

4 cups/200g stale breadcrumbs

a little salt and freshly ground black pepper

2 free-range eggs

a little hot stock

For the gravy

goose neck, chopped

goose wings

1 carrot, roughly chopped

1 onion, roughly chopped

giblets

2 bay leaves

6 peppercorns

1 tablespoon all-purpose/plain flour

TO SERVE

potatoes and/or root vegetables, for roasting alongside the goose

unsweetened apple sauce/stewed apple

SERVES 8–10

Preheat the oven to 400°F/200°C/Gas 6.

Chop off the wings and keep these for the stock. Pull out all the fat from inside the bird and cut off any extra visible fat. (Melt this fat gently in a saucepan, then strain it through a fine strainer/sieve or muslin. Keep in a jar in the fridge to roast vegetables or lean meat, such as rabbit.)

To make the stuffing, sweat the onions in a little of the goose fat until they are translucent. Add the sage, breadcrumbs, and seasoning, and bind with the eggs and a few spoonfuls of hot stock—the mixture should be moist enough to bind together but not at all sloppy. You can cook the stuffing separately if you prefer (see page 16 for instructions). If you are using it to stuff the goose, you will need to weigh the stuffing first.

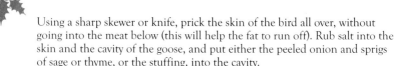

Using a sharp skewer or knife, prick the skin of the bird all over, without going into the meat below (this will help the fat to run off). Rub salt into the skin and the cavity of the goose, and put either the peeled onion and sprigs of sage or thyme, or the stuffing, into the cavity.

To calculate the cooking time, add the weight of the stuffing to the weight of the bird if you are cooking the two together; cook for 15 minutes per 1 lb/450g plus 15 minutes; add 30 minutes' resting time.

Place the goose on a wire rack above a tray and roast in the preheated oven for the required time. Baste from time to time with the fat that collects in the tray. If the goose browns too quickly, cover the breast with foil.

Meanwhile, make the stock for the gravy by frying the chopped neck and wings and vegetables in a little goose fat in a large pan. Pour off any excess fat, add the giblets, bay leaves, and peppercorns and 1¾ pints/1 litre water. Let this simmer for 1½ hours, then strain and set aside.

When you are ready to roast your potatoes and vegetables (about 30 minutes before the goose comes out of the oven), pour out the fat from the tray, leaving enough for roasting (either take the goose out and put it on a board, holding it with two clean dish towels, or put another tray temporarily underneath, so the fat doesn't drip onto the floor of your oven). Continue to roast the goose on the rack with the vegetables in the tray below.

If you are cooking the stuffing separately, place it in a gratin dish and cook in the oven for 30 minutes.

When the goose is cooked through and the juices run clear, transfer it to a large plate, cover with foil, and let it rest for 20–30 minutes before carving.

To make the gravy, thicken the juices in the roasting tray with a little flour over a low heat, and slowly add the strained stock. Pour into a gravy boat.

Serve with unsweetened apple sauce/stewed apple.

ROAST GOOSE WITH SAGE AND ONION STUFFING

When a goose is well picked, singed, and cleaned, make the stuffing with about two ounces of onion and half as much green sage, chop them very fine, adding four ounces, i.e. about a large breakfast-cupful of stale bread-crumbs, a bit of butter about as big as a walnut, and a very little pepper and salt (to this some cooks add half the liver, parboiling it first); the yolk of an egg or two, and incorporating the whole well together, stuff the goose; do not quite fill it, but leave a little room for the stuffing to swell; spit it, tie it on the spit at both ends, to prevent its swinging round, and to keep the stuffing from coming out. From an hour and a half to an hour and three-quarters, will roast a fine full-grown goose. Send up gravy and apple sauce with it.

WILLIAM KITCHINER, *Apicius Redivivus, or The Cook's Oracle*, 1817

ROAST FOWL

There are innumerable roast fowl in Dickens: the working Gargerys in *Great Expectations* have a pair for Christmas dinner, and Flora Casby tries to entice Little Dorrit with a leg of fowl for breakfast. Bella Wilfer in *Our Mutual Friend* insists on cooking them for her parents' anniversary dinner, twirling them on the spit so fast that they are pink inside. Alexis Soyer's lovely recipe is here adapted to pot-roasting, which suits modern-day chickens better than boiling.

2¾–3¼ lb/1.25–1.5kg free-range chicken

½ a lemon

a few sprigs of tarragon, plus 30–40 leaves

2 slices of unsmoked streaky bacon

oil, for frying

2 onions, thickly sliced

2 or 3 carrots, thickly sliced

1 or 2 turnips, thickly sliced

2 sticks of celery

2 bay leaves

a few sprigs of thyme

a wineglass of sherry or 2–3 glasses of white wine, plus enough stock to make about 2¼ cups/500ml liquid

salt, freshly ground black pepper, and nutmeg, to season

SERVES 4

Preheat the oven to 350°F/180°C/Gas 4.

Rub the skin of the chicken all over with the half lemon, then put the lemon in the bird's cavity with the sprigs of tarragon. Season the chicken inside and out with a little salt, pepper, and nutmeg.

Chop the bacon and fry quickly in a very little oil in the bottom of a large casserole. Add the onions and fry until they are beginning to soften.

Add the remaining vegetables, turn them in the oil, and let them sweat for a minute or two. Add the bay leaves, thyme, and sherry or wine, and bring to the boil; bubble for a moment, then add the stock and bring back to the boil, then turn off the heat.

Place the chicken on top of the vegetables. Put a lid on and put in the oven. Cook for 1 hour with the lid on, then remove it and cook for another 30-45 minutes, to brown the chicken skin.

When it is cooked through and the juices run clear, take the chicken out of the casserole and keep warm.

Strain the cooking juices into a small pan and reduce to thicken. Add the tarragon leaves and serve the gravy separately.

CAPON OR POULARD A L'ESTRAGON

I have been told many fanciful epicures idolize this dish. The bird should be trussed for boiling. Rub the breast with half a lemon, tie over it some thin slices of bacon, cover the bottom of a small stewpan with thin slices of the same, and a few trimmings of either beef, veal, or lamb, two onions, a little carrot, turnip and celery, two bay-leaves, one sprig of thyme, a glass of sherry, two quarts of water, season lightly with salt, pepper, and nutmeg, simmer about one hour and a quarter, keeping continually a little fire on the lid, strain three parts of the gravy into a small basin, skim off the fat, and pass through a tammy into a small stewpan, add a drop of gravy or colouring to give it a nice brown colour, boil a few minutes longer, and put about forty tarragon leaves; wash, and put it in the boiling gravy, with a tablespoonful of good French vinegar, and pour over the capon when you serve it; it is an improvement to clarify the gravy. All kinds of fowls and chickens are continually cooked in this manner in France. They are also served with rice.

ALEXIS SOYER, *The Modern Housewife or Ménagère,* 1849

MASHED AND BROWN POTATOES

In spite of the disastrous potato blight in the 1840s and the resulting famine in Ireland, "a dish of potatoes" was still demanded for English tables such as the Casbys. Catherine Dickens served them at nearly every meal, frequently "mashed and brown," made from what Margaret Dods admired as the Scottish and Irish "dry farinaceous" variety of potato; rather than the "cheesy, waxy roots" that she believed Londoners relished.

2 lb/900g floury potatoes, peeled and quartered, eyes and discolored parts cut out

2 tablespoons milk or heavy/double cream

½ cup/100g butter, plus extra for baking

1 egg, beaten

salt

SERVES 4

Preheat the oven to 400°F/200°C/Gas 6.

Cook the potatoes in a pan of salted boiling water until you can easily pierce them with the point of a knife. Drain well and return the pan to a low heat for a few seconds to make sure the potatoes are dry; add the milk or cream and the butter and when it has melted, mash well. It helps to do this over a very low heat, but don't let the bottom of the pan burn. Don't over-mash or they will become gluey.

Spoon or pipe the mashed potato into a gratin dish, or individual dishes or scallop shells. Brush with beaten egg and dot with butter.

Bake for 15–30 minutes (depending on the size of the dish) until the top is well browned.

MASHED AND BROWN POTATOES

Mashed Potatoes may be pressed into patty pans previously buttered, and turned out and browned; or put into stoneware scallop-shell shapes, glazed with eggs, and browned before the fire, sticking a few bits of butter upon them. A few of these make a pretty supper-dish.

MARGARET DODS, *The Cook and Housewife's Manual,* 1826

CAULIFLOWER WITH PARMESAN

Although Smallweed and co. eschew the "artificially whitened cauliflowers" in favor of summer cabbage (without slugs) in *Bleak House*, Catherine's light version of cauliflower cheese makes a sophisticated side vegetable with hollandaise, rather than the usual gloopy white sauce. She probably enjoyed it on the family's sojourns in France, Italy, or Switzerland.

1 large cauliflower

7 tablespoons/100g unsalted butter

2 US extra-large/ UK large fresh, free-range egg yolks

1 tablespoon lemon juice

salt and freshly ground white pepper

a pinch of nutmeg

⅔ cup/50g grated Parmesan

SERVES 6–8 AS A SIDE DISH

Preheat the oven to 375°F/190°C/Gas 5.

Cut the cauliflower into florets (keeping the stems on) and boil or steam them until just tender. Drain and reassemble them into their cauliflower shape in a deep dish or bowl.

To make the sauce, melt the butter in a small pan. Put the egg yolks in a heatproof bowl over a pan of simmering water and whisk in the lemon juice. Whisk in the melted butter a very little at a time, keeping the whisking going all the time so the sauce does not separate (you may like to use a blender). The yolks will thicken as they cook, giving you a pouring consistency. Season with salt, white pepper, and a tiny rasp of nutmeg.

Pour the sauce over the reassembled cauliflower and sprinkle the Parmesan on the top. (The hollandaise is so rich that I've suggested using very little Parmesan, although Catherine's was a cheese-loving family and it sounds as if she used more.)

Bake in the preheated oven for 20 minutes.

TO BOIL CAULIFLOWER WITH PARMESAN

Boil a cauliflower, drain it on a sieve, and cut it into convenient-sized pieces, arrange these pieces in a pudding-basin so as to make them resemble a cauliflower on the dish, season it as you proceed, turn it on the dish, then cover it with a sauce made of grated parmesan cheese, butter, and the yolks of a couple of eggs seasoned with lemon juice, pepper, salt, and nutmeg, and put parmesan grated over it; bake for twenty minutes and brown it.

CATHERINE DICKENS, *What Shall We Have for Dinner?*, 1851

A YORKSHIRE CHRISTMAS PIE

The appetite of the bluff Yorkshireman John Browdie is a running joke in **Nicholas Nickleby**. The breakfast that Nicholas shares with him on a winter morning includes "Yorkshire pie, and other cold substantials." Yorkshire pies were made at Christmas, often as gifts, and featured birds of a succession of sizes, from turkey down to partridge, boned and stuffed inside each other. Few modern ovens are big enough for this, but the recipe is fascinating.

A YORKSHIRE CHRISTMAS-PYE

First make a good Standing Crust, let the Wall and Bottom be very thick, bone a Turkey, a Goose, a Fowl, a Partridge, and a Pigeon, season them all very well, take half an Ounce of Mace, half an Ounce of Nutmegs, a quarter of an Ounce of Cloves, half an Ounce of black Pepper, all beat fine together, two large Spoonfuls of Salt, mix them together.

Open the Fowls all down the Back, and bone them; first the Pigeon, then the Partridge, cover them; then the Fowl, then the Goose, and then the Turkey, which must be large; season them all well first, and lay them in the Crust, so as it will look only like a whole Turkey; then have a Hare ready cased, and wiped with a clean Cloth. Cut it to Pieces, that is jointed; season it, and lay it as close as you can on one Side; on the other Side Woodcock, more Game, and what Sort of wild Fowl you can get. Season them well, and lay them close; put at least four Pounds of Butter into the Pye, then lay on your Lid, which must be a very thick one, and let it be well baked. It must have a very hot Oven, and will take at least four Hours.

This Pye will take a Bushel of Flour; in this Chapter, you will see how to make it. These Pies are often sent to London in a Box as Presents; therefore the Walls must be well built.

HANNAH GLASSE, *The Art of Cookery Made Plain and Easy*, 1747

PICKLED PORK

Pork legs, such as the one that Pip's ferocious sister serves at their Christmas dinner in *Great Expectations*, were often pickled with dry salt which enabled them to keep for many months. Hannah Glasse's recipe for a wet cure is easier to do and could be used in two ways. Season roast pork by leaving the leg in the pickle overnight, before drying and roasting as usual. Alternatively, pickle it for about a week to make a beautiful Christmas ham that can be braised and then eaten hot or cold.

1 half leg of pork (weighing about 6½ lb/3kg)

For the pickle

5 pints/3 litres water (substitute 1 quart/1 litre with hard/strong cider or ale if you wish)

14 oz/400g curing salt (i.e. salt with the right proportion of sodium nitrite, which keeps it pink)

1¾ cups/350g dark soft brown sugar or molasses/black treacle

plus any of the following optional flavorings:

a small bunch of thyme

3 sprigs of rosemary

4 bay leaves

2 tablespoons juniper berries or allspice berries, slightly crushed

a fragment of nutmeg

2 teaspoons cloves

2 teaspoons black peppercorns, slightly crushed

To boil the pickled pork

stock vegetables, such as 1 large peeled onion, 2 roughly chopped carrots, and 2 roughly chopped parsnips

2 bay leaves

a small bunch of parsley stalks

a small bunch of chives

a sprig of thyme

a sprig of marjoram

10 peppercorns

For the glaze

2 tablespoons honey or soft brown sugar

1 tablespoon English or French mustard, or to taste

1½ cups/50g day-old breadcrumbs

SERVES 12–16

To make the pickle, bring the water, cider or ale (if using), salt, and sugar or molasses/treacle to the boil in a non-corrosive saucepan (stainless steel is fine); make sure it doesn't boil over. Skim the scum from the surface, then add the herbs and spices, making sure the salt and sugar dissolve. Let the pickling brine cool completely. When cold, you can check that it's salty enough by floating a fresh egg on the surface!

Put the pork in a large, non-metallic container, such as a bowl or food-grade bucket. Strain the brine over, making sure it covers the meat; you could weigh down the meat with a plastic weight or some upturned soup bowls. Cover and refrigerate or store at 43–46°F/6–8°C.

Either take the pork out of the brine the following day, rinse, and let it dry before roasting as normal, or leave it soaking in the brine for 5–7 days. Check the brine every day—if it begins to smell off, discard it, and cover the meat with fresh brine.

The day before you want to cook the pork, remove it from the brine, rinse, and dry with kitchen paper. Hang the pork in a cold, dry, airy place if you can for 24 hours. If not, wrap it in a clean cotton cloth and keep in the fridge.

To boil the pork, place it in a large pan of cold water and bring it to the boil; if the water tastes salty, discard it, replace with fresh cold water, and repeat until the cooking water tastes only lightly salted. Then add the stock vegetables, herbs, and seasonings to the pan and simmer the meat very gently for 22–27 minutes per 1 lb or 25–30 minutes per 500g. Skim any scum from the surface. Remove from the heat and leave the meat to cool in the cooking liquid for 15–20 minutes.

Preheat the oven to 400°F/200°C/Gas 6.

Peel away the skin from the meat, leaving the fat, and place the meat in a large roasting pan. Score the fat in a diamond pattern, mix the honey or sugar and mustard together, spread this glaze evenly over, and cover with the breadcrumbs. Bake in the preheated oven for 15–20 minutes to crisp the breadcrumbs. Cover and let it stand for 15–20 minutes before carving, or eat it cold.

A PICKLE FOR PORK, WHICH IS TO BE EAT SOON

You must take two Gallons of Pump-water, one Pound of Bay-salt, one Pound of coarse Sugar, six Ounces of Salt-petre, boil it all together, and skim it when cold. Cut the Pork in what Pieces you please, lay it down close, and pour the Liquor over it. Lay a Weight on it to keep it close, and cover it close from the Air, and it will be fit to use in a Week. If you find the Pickle begins to spoil, boil the Pickle again, and skim it; when it is cold, pour it on your Pork again.

HANNAH GLASSE, *The Art of Cookery Made Plain and Easy*, 1747

TO DRESS A HAM A LA BRAISE

Clear the Knuckle, take off the Swerd, and lay it in Water to freshen; then tye it about with a String, take Slices of Bacon and Beef, beat and season them well with Spice and Sweet Herbs; then lay them in the Bottom of a Kettle with Onions, Parsnips, and Carrots sliced, with some Cives [sic] and Parsley; Lay in your Ham the Fat Side uppermost, and cover it with Slices of Beef, and over that Slices of Bacon; then lay on some sliced Roots and Herbs, the same as under it; Cover it close, and stop it close with Paste, put Fire both over and under it, and let it stew with a very slow Fire twelve Hours; put it in a Pan, drudge it well with grated Bread, and brown it with a hot Iron; then serve it up on a clean Napkin, garnished with raw Parsley.

HANNAH GLASSE, *The Art of Cookery Made Plain and Easy*, 1747

LEICESTERSHIRE PORK PIE

In *Great Expectations*, Pip steals a "beautiful round compact pork pie" which was intended for the Christmas dinner. Pork Pies from Melton Mowbray in Leicestershire are still famous for being raised by hand, made with fresh pork, a tiny drop of anchovy essence to help flavor the meat, and jellied stock. In his recipe of 1846, Francatelli omits the anchovy and the stock, but Dorothy Hartley's *Food in England* (published in 1954) reinstates them.

For the pork jelly

2 lb 3 oz/1kg pork bones

2 pig's trotters (ask your butcher to split them)

1 onion, roughly chopped

2 carrots, roughly chopped

1 bouquet garni (or a truss of sage and marjoram)

some apple cores (the pips add a slightly almond flavor and a little acid)

or, instead of all the above ingredients, 3 gelatine leaves and 1¼ cups/300ml well-flavored stock

For the filling

approx. 1 lb 9 oz/700g boned shoulder of pork (keep the bone for the stock)

approx. 2 oz/50g belly of pork

approx. 2 oz/50g unsmoked bacon

3 sage leaves, very finely chopped

1 teaspoon thyme or marjoram leaves, very finely chopped

1 teaspoon anchovy essence

¼ teaspoon grated nutmeg or ground mace

salt and freshly ground white pepper

For the pastry

¾ cup plus 2 tablespoons/200g lard

1 cup/220ml water or milk, or a mix of half and half

4 cups/575g strong all-purpose/plain white flour

1 teaspoon salt

1 egg, beaten, to glaze

You will need a wooden pie dolly or a jam jar

MAKES 6

If making your own jelly, put the pork jelly ingredients in a stockpot with 2–3 quarts/2–3 litres of water. Just cover with water, bring to the boil, and simmer, partially covered, for about 4 hours. Skim off any scum from the surface from time to time. Let it cool a little and strain it through a strainer/sieve.

Reduce the stock to about 1¼ cups/300ml by leaving it on a rolling boil in an uncovered pan—the wider the pan, the better.

Prepare the filling. Chop the pork shoulder into cubes about ½ inch/ 1cm square or smaller (a meat cleaver is useful for this). Mince or finely chop the pork belly and bacon. Mix these up well with the rest of the filling ingredients. If you aren't sure about the seasoning, fry a little piece in hot oil to taste. You can do this the night before and leave in the fridge to let the flavors develop.

Preheat the oven to 350°F/180°C/Gas 4. Grease a baking tray.

For the pastry, put the lard into a pan with the liquid and heat gently until it is melted and the liquid is hot but not boiling. Sift the flour and salt into a large bowl and make a well in the center. Pour the hot liquid into the well and beat with a wooden spoon until it is well mixed, then knead well until smooth.

Divide the pastry into six equal parts. For each part, pinch off a quarter for the pie lid and roll out the remainder to about ¾ inch/2cm thick. Cover a pie dolly or jam jar in plastic wrap/clingfilm and flour it well; invert it and drape the pastry over, pressing it down the sides until it is about 2–2½ inches/ 5–6cm high. Cut a clean top edge with a knife.

Upturn the jar and carefully ease the dolly or jar and plastic wrap/clingfilm out of the pastry. Pack a sixth of the meat mixture into the pastry, pressing it down so there are no air gaps.

Roll out the top pastry and cut it to the same size as the pie; punch out a small round hole in the center for the air to escape (and the jelly to go in). Place it on top of the meat, inside the edges of the pastry case, and pinch the sides and top together with wet fingers. You can make it more upright by pushing it gently with your cupped hands and turning it, as if it were a pot on a potter's wheel.

Decorate the top of the pie with scraps of pastry. Dorothy Hartley says "Pie art has moved with the times, and the most modern pies have now an austerity of outline. Nevertheless, an acorn or a rosette is suitable, and four oak leaves or a beech-nut in paste show a nice feeling for the pig's previous environment." Brush with the beaten egg. Repeat to make the remaining pies.

Carefully transfer the pies to the greased baking tray. Bake in the preheated oven for about 1 hour 20 minutes, but check them after an hour. If they are browning too quickly, cover with baking parchment paper.

Leave the pies to cool. The filling contracts as they cool, leaving gaps for the jelly to fill.

If you are making jelly from gelatine, soak the leaves in cold water for 10 minutes, then squeeze out the excess water and dissolve the gelatine in the warm stock.

Make sure your stock is just about liquid—somewhere between tepid and warm. Using a funnel, pour it through the hole in the top of each pie. Leave to set overnight in a cool place or in the fridge.

LEICESTERSHIRE PORK PIE

Cut the pork up in square pieces, fat and lean, about the size of a cob-nut, season with pepper and salt, and a small quantity of sage and thyme chopped fine, and set it aside on a dish in a cool place. Next, make some hot-water-paste, using for this purpose (if desired) fresh-made hog's lard instead of butter, in the proportion of eight ounces to the pound of flour. These pies must be raised by hand, in the following manner:-

First mould the paste into a round ball upon the slab, then roll it out to the thickness of half an inch, and with the back of the right hand indent the centre in a circle reaching to within three inches of the edge of the paste; next, gather up the edges all round, pressing it closely with the fingers and thumbs, so as to give to it the form of a purse; then continue to work it upwards, until the sides are raised sufficiently high; the pie should now be placed on a baking-sheet, with a round of buttered paper under it, and after it has been filled with the pork – previously prepared for this purpose, covered in with some of the paste in the usual manner. Trim the edges and pinch it round with the pincers, decorate it, egg it over and bake it until done: calculating the time it should remain in the oven, according to the quantity of meat it contains.

CHARLES ELME FRANCATELLI, *The Modern Cook*, 1846

CHESTNUT AND APPLE MINCE PIES

This old Scottish recipe brings together the chestnuts from the trees around Joe's forge and the mincemeat that went into Mrs. Joe's "handsome mince-pie," made before Pip stole the leftovers for Magwitch. The chestnut paste lightens the mix and gives a delightful toffee-ish taste.

For the pastry
2⅔ cups/350g all-purpose/plain flour
¾ cup/175g cold butter
1 egg yolk
beaten egg or milk, to glaze

For the mincemeat
1 large cooking apple, peeled, cored, and finely chopped (approx. 7 oz/200g)
1 cup/200g cooked chestnuts, finely chopped

6½ tablespoons/80g dark soft brown sugar
1 teaspoon ground cinnamon
2 tablespoons brandy
zest of an orange or clementine
1½ cups/180g mixed raisins, currants, and golden raisins/sultanas
½ cup/60g candied/mixed peel
1 cup/100g suet

MAKES 12 DEEP-FILLED PIES

To make the pastry, sift the flour into a large bowl. Cut the cold butter into small pieces in the flour using a knife, then stir until every piece is coated with flour. Using your fingertips, rub the butter into the flour until it is no longer visible. Add 2 tablespoons iced water to the egg yolk, and stir this into the flour. Mix with the blade of a knife, adding a little more cold water to make it into a stiff paste. Bring it together into a ball with your hands, touching it as little as possible. Cover with plastic wrap/clingfilm, and chill in the fridge for 20–30 minutes or until ready to use.

To make the mincemeat, cook the apple, chestnuts, and sugar together in a very little water for 15–20 minutes until soft and toffee-ish. Purée them together with the cinnamon, brandy, and orange zest. Adjust the flavorings to taste. Allow to cool, then mix in the dried fruit and suet.

Preheat the oven to 400°F/200°C/Gas 6.

Roll out the pastry to about ⅛ inch/3mm thick, and cut into rounds of about 4 inches/10cm to line muffin trays. Fill each pastry case with mincemeat, packing down the mixture.

Roll out the remaining pastry and cut into rounds of about 3¼ inches/ 8cm to form the lids. Crimp them together and seal with beaten egg or milk. Decorate the tops (or replace the lids) with holly leaves, stars, angels, or bells, cut from the pastry trimmings, then brush the surface with beaten egg or milk.

Bake in the preheated oven for about 15–20 minutes until golden.

FOR A CHESTNUT FLORENTIN

Take your apples and peel them and take out the hearts, then take and boil your chestnuts till the skins come of and some orange peel & sedron and cut in small pieces, & synemon, & resons, & white whine & for a peast take a pound of butter and a forpet of flour, and roll it out and some shuggar...

Anonymous Scottish Cookbook Manuscript,
NATIONAL LIBRARY OF SCOTLAND

[forpet = fourth of a peck; sedron = candied citron; peast = paste/pastry]

CHRISTMAS PUDDING

Plum puddings were ideal for special occasions; even the poor who
had no oven could boil one up in the washing copper, like Mrs.
Cratchit. Eliza Acton had almost certainly read *A Christmas Carol*;
two years after it was published she was the first to rename plum
pudding "Christmas Pudding." Her recipe is still recommended by
modern cookery writers for being both light and rich.

1⅔ cups/170g grated suet (ask your
butcher for approx. 7 oz/200g fresh
beef-kidney suet)

⅔ cup/85g all-purpose/
plain flour

a small pinch of salt

1½ cups/85g fresh white breadcrumbs

¾ cup/140g soft brown sugar

½ teaspoon apple pie spice/mixed
spice

1½ cups/170g raisins

1½ cups/170g currants

¾ cup/55g chopped candied/mixed
peel

¾ cup/115g apple, peeled, cored and
roughly grated

3 extra-large (US)/large (UK) eggs,
beaten

⅔ cup/140ml brandy

butter, for greasing

*You will need a 2½-pint/1.5-litre
pudding basin*

SERVES 6–8

Prepare the beef-kidney suet by stripping out the membrane and colored
spots, then grate on the coarse side of your grater, ending up with 1⅔
cups/170g.

Sift the flour and salt together, then mix with the remaining dry ingredients,
the dried fruit, the candied/mixed peel, the grated apple, and the suet.

Beat the eggs and brandy together, then stir the mixture into the dry ingredients. Mix it hard with a wooden spoon; make a wish as you do so.

Grease your pudding basin and line the bottom with a circle of baking parchment paper. Pack the mixture into the basin. Cover with a square of parchment paper or greased greaseproof paper and a pudding cloth or piece of kitchen foil on top; make a pleat in both layers to allow room for expansion during cooking. Tie very tightly with string.

Place the basin in a large pan and pour in enough boiling water to come about halfway up the basin; cover with a lid and steam or boil for 3½ hours, adding more boiling water to the pan as necessary so it doesn't boil dry.

When cooked, remove the paper and cloth or foil from the top of the basin and replace with fresh paper. Keep in a cool, dry place until required.

When ready to eat, steam or boil again for 1½–2 hours. Serve with Punch Sauce (see page 37).

THE AUTHOR'S CHRISTMAS PUDDING

To three ounces of flour, and the same weight of fine, lightly-grated bread-crumbs, add six of beef kidney-suet, chopped small, six of raisins weighed after they are stoned, six of well-cleaned currants, four ounces of minced apples, five of sugar, two of candied orange-rind, half a teaspoonful of nutmeg mixed with pounded mace, a very little salt, a small glass of brandy, and three whole eggs. Mix and beat these ingredients well together, tie them tightly in a thickly-floured cloth, and boil them for three hours and a half. We can recommend this as a remarkable light small rich pudding; it may be served with German wine, or punch sauce.

Flour, 3 oz; bread-crumbs, 3 oz; suet, stoned raisins, and currants, each 6 oz; minced apples, 4 oz; sugar, 5 oz; candied peel, 2 oz; spice, ½ teaspoonful; salt, few grains; brandy, small wineglassful; eggs, 3: 3½ hours.

ELIZA ACTON, *Modern Cookery for Private Families*, 1845

PUNCH SAUCE

Eliza Acton suggests serving her pudding with punch sauce.
Warming and intoxicating, punch was, according to Bob Sawyer in
The Pickwick Papers, guaranteed to ward off rheumatism unless
"the patient fell into the vulgar error of not taking enough of it."

1 lemon

2 oranges

¼ cup/50g light brown muscovado sugar

¾ cup/175ml sweet white wine

2 tablespoons rum

2 tablespoons brandy

3 tablespoons/40g unsalted butter

2 teaspoons all-purpose/plain flour

Pare the zest in strips from half the lemon and half an orange, taking care that you don't get any of the bitter white pith. Squeeze the juice from both oranges and from half the lemon. Put the strips of zest in a pan with the sugar and ⅓ cup/150ml water. Simmer them gently for 15–20 minutes, then remove and discard the zest.

Add the juices, the wine, rum, and brandy and heat gently but do not allow it to boil.

Blend the butter and flour together until you have a smooth paste. Add this, about a teaspoonful at a time, to the liquid, whisking well after each addition. As the butter melts into the sauce, the flour will thicken it.

Keep the sauce hot, but below boiling point, and serve in a warm pitcher/jug.

PUNCH SAUCE FOR SWEET PUDDINGS

With two ounces of sugar and a quarter of a pint of water, boil very gently the rind of half a small lemon, and somewhat less of orange-peel, from fifteen to twenty minutes; strain out the rinds, thicken the sauce with an ounce and a half of butter and nearly a teaspoonful of flour, add a half-glass of brandy, the same of white wine, two-thirds of a glass of rum, with the juice of half an orange, and rather less of lemon-juice; serve the sauce very hot, but do not allow it to boil after the spirit is stirred in.

Sugar, 20 oz; water, ¼ pint; lemon and orange-rind; 14 to 20 minutes. Butter, 1½ oz; flour, 1 teaspoonful; brandy and white wine, each ½ wineglassful; rum, two-thirds of glassful; orange and lemon-juice.

ELIZA ACTON, *Modern Cookery for Private Families*, 1845

MR. DICK'S GINGERBREAD

Betsey Trotwood directs David Copperfield to open an account at a cake shop so that the childlike Mr. Dick might be treated to his favorite gingerbread on credit—but only up to one shilling per day. Both cake and biscuit gingerbreads were traditionally decorated as Christmas treats and the cloves in Eliza Acton's recipe hark back to the gilded cloves that ornamented medieval gingerbread.

4 eggs

4 tablespoons milk

scant 3½ cups/450g self-rising flour

1 heaped tablespoon ground ginger (ground ginger loses its flavor rapidly, so buy in small quantities and use up quickly)

1 teaspoon ground cloves

⁷/₈ cup/280g molasses/black treacle

⁷/₈ cup/280g corn syrup/golden syrup

¾ cup plus 2 tablespoons/175g soft brown or muscovado sugar

¾ cup/170g butter, plus extra for greasing

zest of 2 lemons or oranges

2–3 tablespoons chopped stem ginger (optional)

SERVES 10–12

Preheat the oven to 325°F/170°C/Gas 3. Grease and line a 9-inch/23-cm square cake pan/tin.

Whisk the eggs thoroughly with the milk, until they start to froth. Sift the flour and spices into a large bowl. Measure the molasses/black treacle and syrup into a saucepan (this is easiest to do using a metal spoon heated in hot water). Add the sugar, butter, and zest. Heat very gently until the butter is just melted. Pour this into a well in the flour, beating vigorously. When it is well blended, add the egg and milk mixture and the stem ginger, if using, beating well until you can see bubbles forming on the surface.

Pour into the prepared cake pan/tin and bake in the preheated oven for about 1½ hours until firm to the touch and a skewer inserted into the center comes out clean. Turn out and cool on a wire rack. Store in an airtight container or wrapped in foil for a day or two before eating to let the flavors develop.

ACTON GINGERBREAD

Whisk four strained or well-cleared eggs to the lightest possible froth and pour to them, by degrees, a pound and a quarter of treacle, still beating them lightly. Add, in the same manner, six ounces of pale brown sugar free from lumps, one pound of sifted flour, and six ounces of good butter, just sufficiently warmed to be liquid, and no more, for if hot, it would render the cake heavy; it should be poured in small portions to the mixture, which should be well beaten up with the back of a wooden spoon as each portion is thrown in: the success of the cake depends almost entirely on this part of the process. When properly mingled with the mass, the butter will not be perceptible on the surface; and if the cake be kept light by constant whisking; large bubbles will appear in it to the last. When it is so far ready, add to it one ounce of Jamaica ginger and a large teaspoonful of cloves in fine powder, with the lightly grated rinds of two fresh full-sized lemons.

Butter thickly, in every part, a shallow square tin pan, and bake the gingerbread slowly for nearly or quite an hour in a gentle oven. Let it cool a little before it is turned out, and set it on its edge until cold, supporting it, if needful, against a large jar or bowl. We have usually had it baked in an American oven, in a tin less than two inches deep; and it has been excellent. We retain the name given to it originally in our own circle.

ELIZA ACTON, Modern Cookery for Private Families, 1845

TWELFTH CAKE

Charles and Catherine's first son, Charley, was born on Twelfth Night (January 6) and every year his godmother, Angela Burdett-Coutts, would send a huge Twelfth Cake for his birthday. One cake followed the Dickens family to Genoa, where a Swiss pastry cook repaired a chip in its highly decorative frosting and displayed it in his window for the townsfolk to admire. In 1870 Queen Victoria, believing it was too rowdy, had the feast of Twelfth Night removed from the holiday calendar, and the cake migrated to Christmas.

3 cups/400g all-purpose/plain flour

1 teaspoon grated nutmeg

½ teaspoon ground cinnamon

¼ teaspoon ground allspice

¼ teaspoon ground mace

¼ teaspoon ground ginger

¼ teaspoon ground coriander

a pinch of salt

1½ cups plus 2 teaspoons/350g butter, softened, plus extra for greasing

1¾ cups/350g soft brown sugar or golden granulated/caster sugar

grated zest of ½ lemon

6 US extra large/UK large free-range eggs, beaten

2 tablespoons brandy

7½ cups/1kg currants (or 4½ cups/600g currants and 1½ cups/200g each raisins and golden raisins/sultanas)

1½ cups/200g cut candied/mixed peel (or ¾ cup/100g peel and ¾ cup/100g candied citron, if you can find it)

1 cup/100g almonds, chopped or flaked

For the almond paste

4½ cups/450g ground almonds

3 cups/350g confectioners'/icing sugar, sifted

approx. 2 tablespoons liquid, such as orange or lemon juice, orange-flower water, brandy, or liqueur

or, instead of the separate ingredients, 1¾ lb/800g store-bought white almond paste/marzipan

For the frosting

2 lb/900g royal icing sugar

7 tablespoons water

blue food coloring

white fondant decorations

You will need a deep round cake pan/tin 9 inches/23cm in diameter, plus molds for the decorations. Also, for the sake of tradition, a ceramic bean and a ceramic pea

SERVES ABOUT 20

Preheat the oven to 300°F/150°C/Gas 2. Grease and line the cake pan/tin, using a double thickness of greaseproof paper.

Sift the flour and spices into a large bowl with a pinch of salt.

Put the softened butter, sugar, and lemon zest into a bowl and beat together until pale and fluffy. Add the beaten eggs a very little at a time; sprinkle in a spoonful of the flour if the mixture begins to separate. Beat in the brandy. Fold in the flour using a metal spoon, followed by the fruit, peel, and nuts.

To make it a proper Twelfth Cake, hide a ceramic bean and pea in the mixture. Whoever finds them in their slice becomes the King and Queen (respectively) of the Twelfth Night celebrations.

Spoon the mixture into the prepared cake pan/tin and bake in the preheated oven for 2½ hours. Cover the top of the cake with paper if it is browning too quickly. Turn the oven down to 275°F/140°C/Gas 1 for a further 1½ hours. Check the cake after it has been in the oven for 3½ hours—it is done when a skewer inserted into the middle comes out clean. Let the cake cool a little and then turn it out of the pan and cool on a wire rack.

To make your own almond paste, mix the ground almonds in a bowl with the sifted confectioners'/icing sugar; add the liquid little by little and mix well until you have a pliable dough that isn't too sticky to roll out.

To cover the cold cake with the almond paste or marzipan, roll it out to ⅛–¼ inch/3–5mm thick. Using your cake pan/tin as a guide, cut out a circle for the top. Cut three lengths of 9½ inches/24cm for the sides. Place on and around the cake, then smooth the joins together with warm water. Let the almond paste dry.

For the frosting, sift the sugar into the bowl of an electric mixer, sprinkle the water over the top, and beat slowly at first, to avoid clouds of sugar. When it is combined, add blue coloring drop by drop and continue to beat until it is the desired mid-blue color.

Ice the cake with two coats of blue royal icing, letting the first one dry overnight. Decorate with white fondant icing decorations, such as fleur de lys and crowns on top for the king and queen.

TWELFTH CAKE

Two pounds of sifted flour, two pounds of sifted loaf sugar, two pounds of butter, eighteen eggs, four pounds of currants, one half pound of almonds blanched and chopped, one half pound of citron, one pound of candied orange and lemon-peel cut into thin slices, a large nutmeg grated, half an ounce of ground allspice; ground cinnamon, mace, ginger, and corianders, a quarter of an ounce of each, and a gill of brandy.

Put the butter into a stew-pan, in a warm place, and work it into a smooth cream with the hand, and mix it with the sugar and spice in a pan (or on your paste board) for some time; then break in the eggs by degrees, and beat it at least twenty minutes; stir in the brandy, and then the flour, and work it a little; add the fruit, sweetmeats, and almonds, and mix all together lightly; have ready a hoop cased with paper, on a baking-plate; put in the mixture, smooth it on the top with your hand, dipped in milk; put the plate on another, with sawdust between, to prevent the bottom from colouring too much: bake it in a slow oven four hours or more, and when nearly cold, ice it with Icing for Twelfth or Bride Cake.

ICING FOR TWELFTH OR BRIDE CAKE

Take one pound of double-refined sugar, pounded and sifted through a lawn sieve; put into a pan quite free from grease; break in the whites of six eggs, and as much powder blue as will lie on a sixpence; beat it well with a spattle for ten minutes; then squeeze in the juice of a lemon, and beat it till it becomes thick and transparent. Set the cake you intend to ice in an oven or warm place five minutes; then spread over the top and sides with the mixture as smooth as possible. If for a wedding-cake only, plain ice it; if for a twelfth cake, ornament it with gum paste, or fancy articles of any description.

Obs. -A good twelfth cake, not baked too much, and kept in a cool dry place, will retain its moisture and eat well, if twelve months old.

WILLIAM KITCHINER, Apicius Redivivus, or The Cook's Oracle, 1817

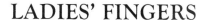

LADIES' FINGERS

Also known as savoy biscuits, Savoiardi, and sponge fingers, these are
the unecclesiastical-sounding "various slender ladies' fingers, to be
dipped into sweet wine and kissed" that the Reverend Septimus'
mother finds in her most wonderful closet in those wintry,
atmospheric days before Christmas in *The Mystery of Edwin Drood*.
Traditionally piped into fingers and used for Charlotte Russe (see
page 50), they can also be piped into loose shapes.

¾ cup/150g granulated/caster sugar

zest of 1 lemon

4 eggs, separated

1 cup plus 2 tablespoons/150g
all-purpose/plain flour

a pinch of cream of tartar (or a few
drops of lemon juice)

½ teaspoon baking powder

2–3 tablespoons golden superfine/
caster sugar, for sprinkling

MAKES ABOUT 20

Preheat the oven to 380°F/190°C/Gas 5. Line three baking trays with baking
parchment paper.

Add the sugar and lemon zest to the egg yolks. Beat well until pale gold. Sift
the flour into the egg yolks and fold in well.

Add the cream of tartar to the egg whites and whisk until stiff (the acid in
the cream of tartar helps them keep their stiffness—if you don't have it, you
could use a few drops of lemon juice); fold them into the yolk mixture.

Put the mixture into a piping bag fitted with a ¼-inch/5-mm nozzle and pipe
3–4-inch/8–10-cm lengths on the paper. Sprinkle golden caster sugar over
the fingers.

Bake in the preheated oven for 15 minutes until they are pale golden (but
check after 10 minutes as they burn quickly).

Slide a knife under the fingers while they are still hot to make sure they
don't stick to the paper; after they have cooled for 2–3 minutes, transfer to
a wire rack.

Serve with tea or use them for Charlotte Russe (see page 50). Your Ladies'
Fingers will probably be flatter and softer than the store-bought variety
(which are made in molds). If you are using them for a Charlotte Russe, you
may wish to line them up on a board and trim them so they are all the same
width and length; although it doesn't look quite as pretty, this makes the
Charlotte Russe easier to assemble.

SAVOY BISCUITS OR CAKES

Ingredients – 4 eggs, 6 oz of pounded sugar, the rind of 1 lemon, 6 oz of flour.

Mode – Break the eggs into a basin, separating the whites from the yolks; beat the yolks well, mix with them the pounded sugar and grated lemon-rind, and beat these ingredients together for ¼ hour. Then dredge in the flour gradually, and when the whites of the eggs have been whisked to a solid froth, stir them to the flour, &c; beat the mixture well for another 5 minutes, then draw it along in strips upon thick cartridge paper to the proper size of the biscuit, and bake them in rather a hot oven; but let them be carefully watched, as they are soon done, and a few seconds over the proper time will scorch and spoil them. These biscuits, or ladies'-fingers, as they are called, are used for making Charlotte Russes, and for a variety of fancy sweet dishes.

Time – 5 to 8 minutes, in a quick oven.

Average cost – 1s, 8d, per lb, or ½d each.

MRS. BEETON'S *Book of Household Management*, 1861

Ladies' Fingers 45

ORANGE AND REDCURRANT JELLIES

Victorian jelly-making was elaborate. The jellies (jello) for Mr. and Mrs. Dombey's ill-starred wedding breakfast were glamorous and grown-up party pieces, not like today's commercial ones served as children's party food. Francatelli's orange boats filled with zestful jelly are an entertaining way to serve the traditional Yorkshire Christmas orange jelly. His striped or "Panachee" jelly, wonderfully vibrant in taste and color, is a featherweight alternative to Christmas pud.

Orange Jelly

7 oranges

½ cup/100g granulated sugar

⅔ cup/150ml cold water

orange juice from a carton (if required)

7 sheets platinum grade gelatine

You will need a jelly bag or muslin

SERVES 4-6

Halve six oranges, gently squeeze out most of the juice with a squeezer, and set aside.

Remove the white pith and remaining pulp from the halved oranges using a teaspoon or grapefruit spoon, taking care not to damage the peel. Do not remove the stalk or you'll have a little hole; if you get this, plug it with kitchen paper. Set the 12 orange halves in muffin pans to keep them level.

Make the orange jelly. Pare the rind from the remaining orange, making sure you have just orange rind and no white pith; then squeeze this and add the juice to the rest. Gently heat the sugar and water together until you have a syrup; don't let it boil. Add the orange rind and leave to cool until it is lukewarm.

Meanwhile, squeeze or liquidize the orange pulp (if you liquidize it, make sure you've taken all the pips out first) to extract all the juice, then discard the pulp. Measure the total amount of orange juice—you will need 2½ cups/ 600ml so add more orange juice from a carton if necessary.

Soak the gelatine leaves in cold water until they have swollen and gone wrinkly (about 6–8 minutes, but no more than 10 minutes or the gelatine starts to disintegrate; also make sure that the leaves don't stick together).

Remove the orange rind from the cooled syrup; add the juice to the syrup in the pan and heat very gently to lukewarm. Squeeze the excess water from the

gelatine leaves, add them to the pan of juice and syrup, and stir until dissolved. Let the mixture cool until it is nearly cold but not set.

Pour the cooled orange jelly into six of the orange halves. Leave in the fridge for several hours to set, or in the freezer for about an hour. When the jelly is completely set, cut each half into quarters. Trim off any excess rind with scissors.

Currant and Raspberry Jelly

5 cups/500g redcurrants and 4 cups/500g raspberries, or 2 lb 3 oz/1kg red or black fruit

⅔ cup/150ml cold water

6½–8 tablespoons/80–100g granulated sugar (add another 4 tablespoons/50g for dark fruit and taste throughout)

approx. 6 leaves of platinum grade gelatine

You can make this with any combination of fruit following some rules. Keep red fruits separate from black. Strawberries and raspberries do not need cooking—just adding them to the hot liquid should make them soft enough to squeeze the juice out. Redcurrants, blackcurrants, blackberries, red and black plums (quartered and stoned), and cherries do need some cooking with sugar and water.

Simmer the currants with the water and sugar for 20–30 minutes. Add the raspberries to the hot liquid, pressing them to get the juice out. Add more sugar to taste. Let it cool and then let it drip through a jelly bag or muslin into a bowl, keeping the juice and discarding the pulp (it will take about an hour).

Measure the juice and for every 7 tablespoons/100ml of liquid, use 1 leaf of gelatine. Soak the gelatine in cold water for 6–8 minutes, as on page 46.

Meanwhile, warm the juice to lukewarm; squeeze the excess water out of the gelatine leaves and add them to the liquid. When they have dissolved completely, let the mixture cool until it is nearly cold but not set.

Pour the cool red jelly into the remaining six orange halves. Leave to set as above, then cut each into quarters and trim as on page 47. Serve the red and orange jellies in alternating colors on a plate.

To Make Panachee Jelly

Any remaining liquid can be set as stripes in a small jelly mold; the easiest way to do this is to pour in the first layer and put it into the freezer until ice crystals just form on the top.

Add the next layer of cooled jelly (if it has solidified, you can warm it again, but don't layer it until it is cool or you won't get a nice sharp line between the two colors).

Let the jellies set in the fridge for several hours or overnight (or in the freezer if you are really short of time, but don't let them freeze).

Turn the jelly out by dipping the mold briefly in warm water (not too long or the jelly will start to melt), then clamping a plate on top and inverting it.

ORANGES FILLED WITH TRANSPARENT JELLY

Select half a dozen oranges without specks on the rind, make a hole at the stalk-end with a circular tin cutter, about half an inch in diameter, and then use a small teaspoon to remove all the pulp and loose pitch from the interior; when this is effected, soak the oranges in cold water for about an hour, then introduce the spoon through the aperture, and scrape the insides smooth, and after rincing them again in cold water, set them to drain on a cloth.

Next, stop up any holes that may have been made in them while scooping out the pulp, and set the oranges in some pounded rough ice contained in a deep sautapan; fill three of them with bright pink-orange jelly, and the remainder with plain jelly. When the jelly has become firm, wipe the oranges with a clean cloth, cut each into four quarters, dish them up tastefully on an ornamental pastry-stand, or upon a napkin, and send to table.

CHARLES ELME FRANCATELLI, *The Modern Cook*, 1846

CURRANT AND RASPBERRY JELLY

Pick the stalks from one quart of redcurrants and a pottle of raspberries, then put these into a large basin with half a pound of pounded sugar and a gill of spring water. Bruise them thoroughly, by squeezing them with the back part of the bowl of a wooden spoon against the sides of the basin. Then throw the whole into a beaver jelly bag, and filter the juice, pouring it back into the bag until it runs through perfectly bright. Next add half a pint of clarified syrup, and two ounces of clarified isinglass to the juice, and pour the jelly into a mould placed in rough ice to receive it.

CHARLES ELME FRANCATELLI, *The Modern Cook*, 1846

CHARLOTTE RUSSE

Invented by the French chef Marie-Antoine Carême and quickly adopted by aristocratic chefs, Charlotte Russe was a popular celebration dessert on middle-class tables. In *What Shall We Have for Dinner?*, Catherine Dickens has a recipe with Crème au Marasquin (a rich, set cream flavored with liqueur made from maraschino cherries), whereas Theodore Garrett's recipe adds a good, tart jelly and real fruit as a foil to the rich cream.

1 batch (approx. 18) Ladies' Fingers (see page 44)

2½ cups/600ml dark red liquid jello/jelly (see Currant and Raspberry Jelly on page 48)

fresh fruit to decorate, such as raspberries, strawberries, cherries

For the crème

10 leaves of gelatine

2 scant cups/450ml full-fat/whole milk

1 vanilla bean/pod

5 free-range egg yolks

2 level tablespoons granulated/caster sugar, plus more to taste

3 cups/400g soft berries, puréed (or you could use any stewed and puréed fruit, such as cherries, plums, apricots, apples, gooseberries, or pears)

1 tablespoon fruit liqueur, such as maraschino, framboise, or cassis (optional)

scant 1¾ cups/400ml whipping cream

You will need an 8¾-inch/22-cm diameter springform cake pan/tin. The setting takes several hours, so give yourself plenty of time.

SERVES 10–12

To make the crème

Put the gelatine leaves into plenty of cold water to soak for 8–10 minutes. Put the milk in a saucepan with the vanilla bean/pod, warm it without boiling, and let it infuse for 5 minutes. Whisk the egg yolks and the sugar together in a bowl until thick and pale.

Remove the vanilla and heat the milk to just below boiling. Pour it over the egg yolks and beat with a balloon whisk.

Squeeze excess water from the gelatine leaves and add the leaves to the custard, then return it to the pan and heat very gently until it thickens. Do not boil.

Let it cool a little, then fold in the fruit purée and, if you like, the liqueur. When it is cold but not set, whip the cream and fold it into the custard.

To assemble

Line the cake pan/tin with plastic wrap/clingfilm, then line the pan with the ladies' fingers, sugar side outermost, packing them together as tightly as possible (see page 44 about cutting them to fit).

Fill the center with the crème. Cover with plastic wrap/clingfilm and leave in the fridge to set. This will take at least 3–4 hours.

To add the jello/jelly

Start to make the jello/jelly (see page 48) about 3 hours before you want to add it, so that it is liquid but as cold as possible, without being set, so that it doesn't ooze through the sponge fingers.

You can either pour on half, let it set, then decorate with fruit and add the other half; or pour on all the jello/jelly, let it set, and decorate with fruit at the end. Give the jello/jelly at least another 3 hours in the fridge to set before unmolding.

To unmold

Place the springform pan on a stand so that you can unclip and pull down the outside of the pan. Using the plastic wrap/clingfilm lining, transfer the charlotte onto your serving plate. Cut the plastic wrap/clingfilm away from the sides, then ease it out from underneath. If you wish, tie a decorative ribbon around the sides of the dessert.

CHARLOTTE RUSSE

Put a little warmed jelly at the bottom of a plain round Charlotte-mould, pack it in ice, and when the jelly commences to set decorate that part of the mould with any fruit that may be desired. Pour in more of the warm jelly to cover the fruit and let it set firm. Cut a few savoy biscuits into various shapes, dip them in sweet jelly, and decorate the sides of the mould with them. Put ½ lb of ripe strawberry puree or jam into a basin, and mix in 1 pint of sweet cream and 1oz of dissolved gelatine. Pour this mixture into the cavity in the mould, cover the top over with a tin, pack ice on the top, and let it remain until the whole is set and firm. Turn the Charlotte out of the mould when ready, and serve.

THEODORE GARRETT, *The Encyclopaedia of Practical Cookery*, Volume 3, 1892–94

FRENCH PLUMS

The French Plums that Scrooge sees in the greengrocer's are
"blushed in modest tartness from their highly-decorated boxes"
(which, if "exceedingly ornamental," even Mrs. Beeton concedes
might be put directly on the dining table). Port and cinnamon turn
too-tart plums into a Christmas delight. Candied French plums were
Christmas gifts, but should not be confused with "sugar plums,"
which are, in fact, sugared nuts or seeds.

3 tablespoons water or juice of
1 orange

3 tablespoons port

1 tablespoon soft brown sugar

a cinnamon stick

a small piece of orange or lemon rind

approx. 1 lb 2 oz/500g French plums,
halved and stones removed

SERVES 4

Put the water or orange juice, port, sugar, cinnamon stick, and lemon rind in
a pan and heat gently until the sugar has dissolved and you have a syrup.

Add the plums, cover, and stew gently for 15 minutes.

Serve with cream or custard.

STEWED PLUMS

*Put twelve French plums in a stew-pan, with a spoonful of brown sugar, a gill
of water, a little cinnamon, and some thin rind of a lemon; let them stew
twenty minutes, then pour them in a basin until cold, take them from their
syrup and eat them dry. They are some-times stewed in wine and water, either
port, sherry, or claret.*

ALEXIS SOYER, *The Modern Housewife or Ménagère*, 1849

WASSAIL

In *The Pickwick Papers*, the revelers at Old Wardle's sat down to a "mighty bowl of wassail," an old country drink of hot ale, often thickened with eggs and with roasted apples bobbing in it. It was a drink for Christmas, New Year, or Twelfth Night, particularly in orchard counties, where revelers toasted the apple trees with wassail to bless the new year's crops. Since modern beers become bitter when heated, cider is a good substitute.

1 quart/1 litre strong dry hard cider or scrumpy

2–4 tablespoons brown sugar, according to taste

2–3 tablespoons apple brandy, or more to taste

6 cloves

2 cinnamon sticks

1 small piece of ginger

a little grated nutmeg, or some small pieces of nutmeg

orange and lemon slices

SERVES 6–8

Put all the ingredients into a saucepan and heat very gently for 15–20 minutes. Do not allow the mixture to boil.

When you are ready to serve, fish out the spices and fruit with a strainer/sieve or slotted spoon, then pour the liquid into heatproof cups.

WASSAIL

(This version is called Brown Betty by Richard Cook)

Dissolve a quarter of a pound of brown sugar in one pint of water, slice a lemon into it, let it stand a quarter of an hour, then add a small quantity of pulverized cloves and cinnamon, half a pint of brandy, and one quart of good strong ale; stir it well together, put a couple of slices of toasted bread into it, grate some nutmeg and ginger on the toast, and it is fit for use.

RICHARD COOK, *Oxford Night Caps: A Collection of Receipts for Making Various Beverages Used in the University*, 1827

PUNCH

When Mr Micawber in *David Copperfield* and the two hard-drinking lawyers in *A Tale of Two Cities*, made punch, Dickens showed the fragrance of lemons, the hit of rum, and the steam transforming a room and a mood. Its magic also begins to work on Scrooge in *A Christmas Carol* when he meets The Ghost of Christmas Present who is flanked by "seething bowls of punch, that made the chamber dim with their delicious steam."

peel and juice of 3 unwaxed lemons

5½ oz/150g brown sugar cubes

1⅔ cups/400ml good-quality Jamaican rum

1 cup plus 1 tablespoon/250ml Cognac

4½ cups/1 litre boiling water

You will need a large enamel pan with a lid

SERVES 10–12

Carefully peel the lemons, not including the bitter white pith. Place in the pan and add the sugar, rum, and brandy. Warm gently.

Take a metal ladleful of the warm spirit, set it alight using a long match and holding it over the pan, then carefully pour the flaming liquid back into the pan to inflame the rest of the liquid.

Let the spirits in the pan burn for 3–4 minutes, then extinguish the flame by putting the lid on. If you don't like the idea of flaming spirits in your kitchen, warm the punch to just below boiling and let it simmer for a few minutes to evaporate some of the alcohol.

Add the lemon juice and the boiling water. Let it cool for 5 minutes; taste for sugar and add more if desired. Leave to stand for 15 minutes in a warm place or a low oven. Discard the pieces of lemon peel before ladling the punch into heatproof glasses.

DICKENS' PUNCH

To Mrs Fillonneau,

48, Rue de Courcelles, Eighteenth January, 1847

My Dear Mrs F.

I send you, on the other side, the tremendous document which will make you for ninety years (I hope) a beautiful Punchmaker in more senses than one.

I shall be delighted to dine with you on Thursday. Mr Forster says amen. Commend me to your Lord, and believe me (with respectful compliment to Lord Chesterfield) always,

Faithfully yours,

Charles Dickens

TO MAKE THREE PINTS OF PUNCH

Peel into a very strong common basin (which may be broken, in case of accident, without damage to the owner's peace or pocket) the rinds of three lemons, cut very thin, and with as little as possible of the white coating between the peel and the fruit, attached. Add a double-handfull of lump sugar (good measure), a pint of good old rum, and a large wine-glass full of brandy – if it be not a large claret glass, say two. Set this on fire, by filling a warm silver spoon with the spirit, lighting the contents at a wax taper, and pouring them gently in. Let it burn three or four minutes at least, stirring it from time to time. Then extinguish it by covering the basin with a tray, which will immediately put out the flame. Then squeeze in the juice of the three lemons, and add a quart of boiling water. Stir the whole well, cover it up for five minutes, and stir again.

At this crisis (having skimmed off the lemon pips with a spoon) you may taste. If not sweet enough add sugar to your liking, but observe that it will be a little sweeter presently. Pour the whole into a jug, tie a leather or coarse cloth over the top, so as to exclude the air completely, and stand it in a hot oven ten minutes, or on a hot stove one quarter of an hour. Keep it until it comes to table in a warm place near the fire, but not too hot. If it be intended to stand three or four hours, take half the lemon-peel out, or it will acquire a bitter taste.

The same punch allowed to grow cool by degrees, and then iced, is delicious. It requires less sugar when made for this purpose. If you wish to produce it bright, strain it into bottles through silk.

The proportions and directions will, of course, apply to any quantity.

SMOKING BISHOP

Scrooge tells Bob Cratchit that they will discuss his affairs over a bowl of "Smoking Bishop," a drink chosen over the more common punch (like turkey in preference to goose) because, made with port, it connotes wealth and fine living. The drink was also known as Oxford Bishop; other versions termed Cardinal and Pope substituted (respectively) claret and champagne for the port.

1 whole orange or lemon

16 whole cloves

2 cups plus 2 tablespoons/500ml water

1–2 tablespoons soft brown sugar, or to taste

1 cinnamon stick

2–3 blades of mace

6 allspice berries

¾–1¼-inch/2–3-cm cube of ginger root, peeled

3¼ cups/750-ml bottle of ruby port

juice of ½ an orange or lemon

a little grated nutmeg

SERVES 6–8

Preheat the oven to 400°F/200°C/Gas 6.

Stud the orange or lemon with the cloves and roast it on a baking tray for 20–30 minutes until soft. Don't let it go brown.

Meanwhile, put the water, sugar, and spices into a pan, bring to the boil, then simmer until the water has reduced by half. Add the port, lemon or orange juice, and a little grated nutmeg to taste; heat without boiling.

Serve in a punch bowl with the clove-studded orange or lemon and the spices floating in it.

SMOKING BISHOP

Make several incisions in the rind of a lemon, stick cloves in the incisions, and roast the lemon by a slow fire. Put small but equal quantities of cinnamon, cloves, mace, and all-spice, and a race of ginger, into a saucepan, with half a pint of water; let it boil until it is reduced one half. Boil one bottle of port wine; burn a portion of the spirit out of it, by applying a lighted paper to the saucepan. Put the roasted lemon and spice into the wine; stir it up well, and let it stand near the fire ten minutes. Rub a few knobs of sugar on the rind of a lemon, put the sugar into a bowl or jug, with the juice of half a lemon (not roasted), pour the wine upon it, grate some nutmeg into it, sweeten it to your taste, and serve it up with the lemon and spice floating in it.

Oranges, although not used in Bishop at Oxford, are, as will appear by the following lines written by Swift, sometimes introduced into that beverage:

Fine oranges

Well roasted, with sugar and wine in a cup,

They'll make a sweet Bishop when gentlefolks sup.

RICHARD COOK, *Oxford Night Caps: A Collection of Receipts for Making Various Beverages Used in the University*, 1827

BIBLIOGRAPHY

Cookbooks

I have given the original publication date for each book, although recipes may have been taken from later editions.

Acton, Eliza, *Modern Cookery for Private Families*, 1845

Anon, Eighteenth-century manuscript recipe book, National Library of Scotland, http://digital.nls.uk/107325984

Beeton, Isabella, *The Book of Household Management*, 1861

Cook, Richard, *Oxford Night Caps: A Collection of Receipts for Making Various Beverages Used in the University*, 1827

Dickens, Catherine, pseud. Lady Maria Clutterbuck, *What Shall We Have for Dinner?*, 1851

Francatelli, Charles Elmé, *The Modern Cook*, 1846

Francatelli, Charles Elmé, *A Plain Cookery Book for the Working Classes*, 1852

Garrett, Theodore Francis, ed., *The Encyclopaedia of Practical Cookery* (8 volumes), 1892–94

Glasse, Hannah, *The Art of Cookery Made Plain and Easy*, 1747

Hartley, Dorothy, *Food in England*, 1954

Johnstone, Christian Isobel, pseud. Margaret Dods, *The Cook and Housewife's Manual*, 1826

Kitchiner, William, *Apicius Redivivus, or The Cook's Oracle*, 1817

Soyer, Alexis, *The Modern Housewife or Ménagère*, 1849

Suggested Reading

Dickens, Cedric, *Dining with Dickens*, 1984

The Dickensian, published by the Dickens Fellowship.

Mayhew, Henry, *London Labour and the London Poor* (3 volumes), 1851

Nayder, Lillian, *The Other Dickens: A Life of Catherine Hogarth*, 2010

Rossi-Wilcox, Susan, *Dinner for Dickens: The Culinary History of Mrs Charles Dickens' Menu Books*, 2005

Tomalin, Claire, *Charles Dickens: A Life*, 2011

Charles Dickens' works

Sketches by Boz, 1836
The Pickwick Papers, 1837
Oliver Twist, 1839
Nicholas Nickleby, 1839
The Old Curiosity Shop, 1841
Barnaby Rudge, 1841
American Notes, 1842
A Christmas Carol, 1843
Martin Chuzzlewit, 1844
Pictures from Italy, 1846
Dombey and Son, 1848
David Copperfield, 1850
Bleak House, 1853
Hard Times, 1854
Little Dorrit, 1857
A Tale of Two Cities, 1859
Great Expectations, 1861
Mrs Lirriper's Legacy, 1864
Our Mutual Friend, 1865
The Uncommercial Traveller, 1869
The Mystery of Edwin Drood, 1870
Household Words (ed.), 1850–59
The Letters of Charles Dickens, The British Academy/The Pilgrim Edition, 12 volumes, eds Madeline House and Graham Storey

INDEX OF RECIPES

Betsey Prig's Twopenny Salad 12

cakes and biscuits
    Ladies' Fingers 44–45
    Mr. Dick's Gingerbread 38
    Twelfth Cake 40–43
Cauliflower with Parmesan 22
Charlotte Russe 51–53
Chestnut and Apple Mince Pies 32
Christmas Pudding 34–36

desserts and puddings
    Charlotte Russe 51–53
    Christmas Pudding 34–36
    French Plums 55
    Orange and Redcurrant Jellies
      46–49
    Punch Sauce 37
drinks
    Punch 58–59
    Smoking Bishop 60–61
    Wassail 56

fish and seafood
    Lobster Patties 8–9
    Pickled Salmon 10
French Plums 55
fruit
    Charlotte Russe 51–53
    Chestnut and Apple Mince Pies 32
    French Plums 55
    Orange and Redcurrant Jellies
      46–49

gingerbread
    Mr. Dick's Gingerbread 38
Goose, Roast 15–17

Ladies' Fingers 44–45
Leicestershire Pork Pie 29–31
Lobster Patties 8–9

Mashed and Brown Potatoes 21
Mr. Dick's Gingerbread 38

Orange and Redcurrant Jellies 46–49

pies and pastries
    Chestnut and Apple Mince Pies 32
    Leicestershire Pork Pie 29–31
    Lobster Patties 8–9
    Yorkshire Christmas Pie/Pye 24
Pickled Pork 25–27
Pickled Salmon 10
pork and ham
    Leicestershire Pork Pie 29–31
    Pickled Pork 25–27
poultry
    Roast Fowl 18
    Roast Goose 15–17
    Yorkshire Christmas Pie/Pye 24
Punch 58–59
Punch Sauce 37

Roast Fowl 18
Roast Goose 15–17

Sage and Onion Stuffing 15, 17
salads 13
    Betsey Prig's Twopenny Salad 12
Salmon, Pickled 10
Smoking Bishop 60–61

Twelfth Cake 40–43

vegetables
    Cauliflower with Parmesan 22–23
    Mashed and Brown Potatoes 21
    see also salads

Wassail 56

Yorkshire Christmas Pie/Pye 24

ACKNOWLEDGMENTS

My great thanks to the friends and family who helped me with ideas and editing, recipes, and testing: Margaret Bluman, Isabelle de Cat, Annabel Huxley, Eleanor Koss, Robbie Koss, David Marshall, Claire McElwee, Simone Doctors, Miranda Vogler-Koss, Clem Vogler, Laura Vogler, Julian Vogler, and particularly my mum, Jill Vogler, and my late dad, Jon Vogler.

Thank you to Louisa Price and Frankie Kubicki at the Charles Dickens Museum for their help and interest. Thanks, too, to the talented team at CICO Books, particularly Sally Powell, and Cindy Richards, Penny Craig, and Patricia Harrington; to Gillian Haslam for her editing; and to Ria Osborne, Luis Peral, and Ellie Jarvis for the food photography.